Spy Files

TOP TECHNOLOGY

Adrian Gilbert

Words in **bold** can be found in the glossary on page 30.

Consultant: Clive Gifford
Editor: Amanda Askew
Designer: Lisa Peacock
Picture Researcher: Maria Joannou

Copyright © QEB Publishing, Inc. 2010

Published in the United States by
QEB Publishing, Inc.
3 Wrigley, Suite A
Irvine, CA 92618

www.qeb-publishing.com

Library of Congress Cataloging-in Publication Data

Gilbert, Adrian.
  Top technology / Adrian Gilbert.
    p. cm. -- (QEB spy files)
  Includes index.
  ISBN 978-1-59566-593-5 (Hardback)
  1. Espionage--Juvenile literature. 2. Electronic surveil-
lance--Juvenile literature. I. Title.
  UB270.5.G55 2008
  621.389'28--dc22
                            2008010032

ISBN 978 1 59566 832 5

Printed and bound in China

Contents

Spy aircraft

During the Cold War (1940s until the 1990s), improvements in the design of cameras and aircraft made spy planes possible.

The most famous of these was the American U-2, which flew very long distances at heights of up to 80,000 feet. It carried cameras that could take 4,000 detailed photographs on a single mission. The U-2 was used in 1962 to find Soviet **missile** sites in Cuba.

Top Secret!
The SR-71 could travel at a speed of more than 2,200 miles an hour — flying from New York to London in one hour and 55 minutes.

▲ *The super-fast SR-71 spy plane. Although it weighed 78 tons, it could climb to a height of 84,973 feet.*

The U-2 was followed by the SR-71, which could fly faster and at a greater height, making it safer from enemy missile attack. The SR-71 was very expensive, and by the end of the 1990s it began to be replaced by satellites and **unmanned aircraft**.

THE U-2 DISASTER

In May 1960, a U-2 flying illegally over the **Soviet Union** was hit by a missile, causing it to crash to the ground. The pilot, Francis Gary Powers, managed to safely eject from the aircraft, but he was arrested by the Soviets when he landed.

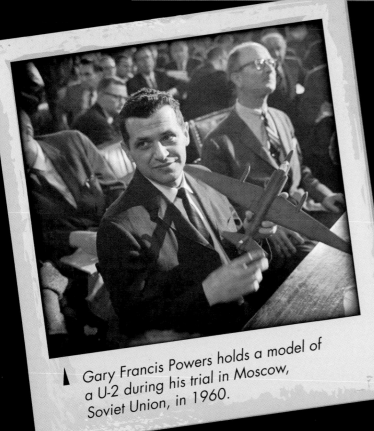

Gary Francis Powers holds a model of a U-2 during his trial in Moscow, Soviet Union, in 1960.

The U.S. **government** denied that its aircraft had flown over the Soviet Union. It thought that the plane had been destroyed and Powers had been killed, so no one would know the truth. However, Soviet leader Nikita Khrushchev told the world that Powers was in their hands and he had already admitted to spying. This caused great embarrassment for the U.S. government. Powers was put in prison. In February 1962, he was returned to the USA in **exchange** for Soviet spy Rudolf Abel.

Soviet leader Nikita Khrushchev examines the wreckage of the crashed U-2.

Spy satellites

The first satellite was launched into space by the Soviet Union in 1957.

A satellite is a machine that is sent into space to orbit Earth, or another planet or moon. It sends back information to Earth. Satellites were soon fitted with cameras with super-powerful lenses that could photograph highly detailed images of the world below.

▼ *The eye in the sky — a U.S. **military** satellite orbits the Earth.*

Top Secret!

Clouds affect many types of satellite. U.S. radar satellites — code-named Lacrosse — can see through heavy clouds and even a short distance underground.

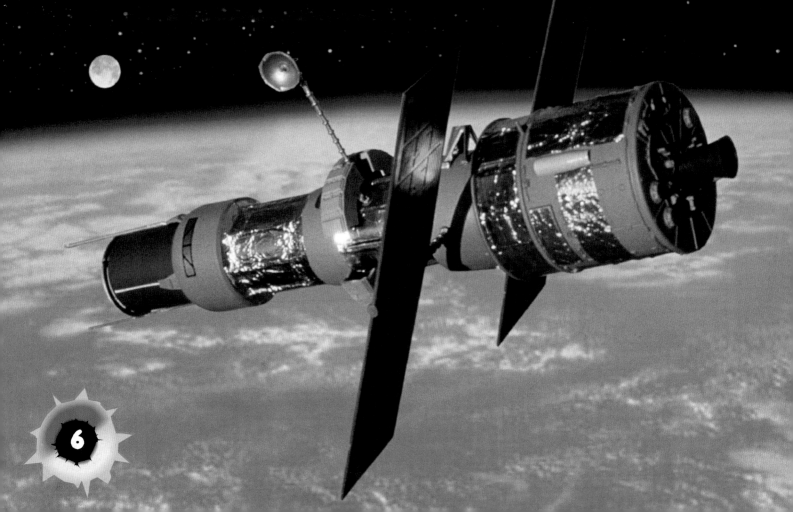

DIGITAL IMAGES

The U.S. KH-11 series — first used in 1976 — changed spying by satellite forever. It did not use film, but instead took digital images that could be sent straight back to Earth. The officers on the ground could then see things as they actually happened.

The next satellite, U.S. KH-12, is thought to have a camera so powerful that it can see objects as small as 6 inches — from space!

KH-11
Launch vehicle: Titan 3D Rocket
Weight: 14.8 tons
Length: 64 feet
Diameter: 10 feet

SLOW SATELLITES

The problem with the early spy satellites was that they had to eject their film in metal cases called canisters. As the canisters fell to Earth by parachute, they could get lost. It might take several days for film to be seen by **intelligence** officers on the ground.

◄ *An amazing level of detail can be seen in this satellite image of the **Capitol Building** in Washington D.C.*

Visual surveillance

Spies spend a lot of time and effort keeping an eye on each other's activities.

Telescopes and binoculars were the first devices to be used for **visual surveillance**. These devices are still used today, along with many others.

► *Not all surveillance equipment is hi-tech. This simple **monocular** is light and easy to carry and still gives good **magnification**.*

CONCEALMENT

Not being seen is very important in spying. As well as night-vision devices, there are folding and miniature monoculars — they hide the fact that the spy is looking at someone. Spies also use concealed surveillance cameras — they take pictures at fixed times, perhaps every 15 seconds. Another device, called the fiberscope, was designed for use in medicine. It has a lens at one end and an eyepiece at the other end. Spies use it to look under a door or through a tiny hole drilled in a wall.

NIGHT-VISION DEVICES

Many spying activities used to be carried out at night because spies were less likely to be watched. Now, special night-vision devices are used so spies can be watched at any time.

Night-vision goggles allow spies to see in the dark. With top night-vision equipment, a spy can see for more than 590 feet.

INFRARED

One type of night-vision device is called infrared. It picks up images of people and objects, and can "see" through fog and smoke as well as in darkness. It does have one weakness—someone using an infrared device can be seen by other people using infrared devices.

The typical green glow of an image intensifier, showing a U.S. Navy helicopter and crewman.

STARLIGHT SCOPES

Another type of night-vision device is called an image intensifier. It uses light — such as starlight or moonlight — to provide a good picture. Often known as a starlight scope, it is invisible to other users and so it is completely secret.

Cameras

The camera is probably the most important piece of equipment that a spy uses.

Cameras are used to take photographs of important military areas, such as airfields and missile sites. They also provide visual identification of important people, as well as copies of documents and plans. There are three broad types of spy camera.

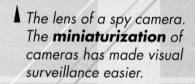

▲ The lens of a spy camera. The **miniaturization** of cameras has made visual surveillance easier.

CONCEALED CAMERAS

A spy must not be seen taking pictures because this can seem suspicious. Special cameras can be fitted into items such as cigarette packets, books or wristwatches, or even within the spy's clothes, with the lens hidden inside a button or tie-pin.

◄ This cigarette lighter contains a concealed camera. It allows the spy to take a photograph without anyone knowing.

SUBMINIATURE CAMERAS

The Minox is the best known subminiature camera—it is a very small camera that can be carried in a pocket, or hidden. Even though they are small, these cameras are strongly built and reliable, and can hold a large film.

Small and reliable, the Minox subminiature camera is still used by spies today.

Top Secret!

The first Minox subminiature camera was produced in Latvia as far back as 1938. It was not made for espionage, but it soon became popular with spies.

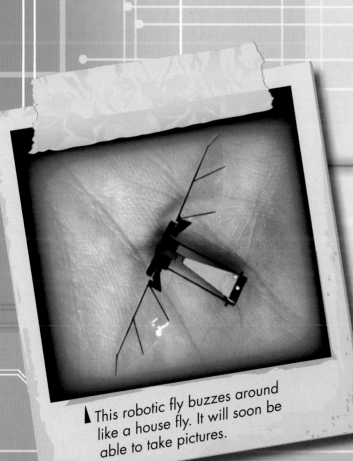

This robotic fly buzzes around like a house fly. It will soon be able to take pictures.

COPY CAMERAS

Spies often have to photograph large numbers of documents within a few minutes. Copy cameras are specially designed to be quick and easy to use.

Eavesdropping, or listening to, the conversations of an enemy is important to a spy.

The invention of tiny listening devices called bugs has made this possible. The bug contains a tiny **microphone** and a **radio transmitter** that sends a signal back to the receiver or records it on tape, a memory chip or memory card.

Top Secret!

In 2001, the Chinese government announced that it had discovered 27 bugs in a Boeing 767 plane that had been bought from the U.S. for President Jiang Zemin.

GOING SMALLER

Bugs are small enough to fit into pens or books, or be disguised as shirt buttons. They are also hidden within pieces of furniture or in electrical sockets. A spy may carry a hidden microphone in his clothes that is connected to a small tape recorder.

◄ A miniature listening device, or a bug. Bugs are getting smaller all of the time, so they can be better hidden.

PHONE TAPS

Bugs can be placed within phone handsets. However, there is a better way of listening to phone conversations — with a **tap**. A special clamp is placed around the phone wire so a person can listen in. Mobile phone calls and computer signals can also be **intercepted**.

▲ A tap is fixed to a telephone in the 1960s. The invention of digital phones has now made this much easier.

BUGGING THE GREAT SEAL

In 1946, Soviet schoolchildren presented a carved wooden copy of the U.S. Great Seal — an emblem used by the U.S. government — to the U.S. Embassy in Moscow, Soviet Union. The seal contained a bug that was only discovered in 1952.

CLEVER DESIGN

The bug was very unusual because it had no power source or transmitter. It took experts some time to realize that nearby sounds — such as a person talking — made a wafer-thin metal disc vibrate inside the bug. These vibrations were picked up by a truck parked close to the Embassy.

▲ The U.S. ambassador reveals the bug placed in the back of the U.S. Great Seal.

Concealment

Spies often carry illegal materials that would prove their guilt if they were to be discovered.

These include stolen documents, as well as the tools of their trade, such as miniature cameras and listening devices. Simple hiding places, such as a space behind a loose brick in a wall, are often the best form of **concealment**.

▲ A reel of **microfilm** is cleverly hidden within this hollowed-out coin. Coins can conceal small objects, such as poison pins.

▼ A hollowed-out book reveals the hiding place for a revolver and ammunition.

ORDINARY OBJECTS

Sometimes a spy will need a normal household item to hide something in. This might be a hole in an ornament or a hollowed-out chess piece. While on the move, a spy might hide material in a can of shaving foam or talcum powder. The list of items is endless, but the spy has to be careful that the object acting as the concealment fits in properly with their way of living.

BOOBY-TRAPPED CONTAINERS

Spy **couriers** spend much of their time carrying film, which may be very important to both sides. To stop the film falling into enemy hands if the courier is caught, intelligence agencies have invented a clever device that destroys the film if it is not opened in the correct way.

Top Secret!

Martha Petersen, a CIA agent working in Moscow, used hollowed-out lumps of coal to pass information to spies working for her in the Soviet Union.

OUT ON A LIMB

Artificial, or false, limbs were common after World War I (1914–1918) because so many men lost arms and legs during the fighting. As a result, spies with artificial limbs found that they made good hiding places. One spy even hid messages behind the eyeball of his artificial eye —he was sure that no one would think to look there!

▲ A reporter shows how microfilm of top-secret military documents was hidden in a pumpkin.

Counter-intelligence devices

As part of counter-intelligence, **spies use many devices to try to stop the activities of enemy spies.**

Listening devices called bugs give off radio signals. If a room is thought to be bugged, it is "swept" by detectors, which will pick up any electronic signals.

INVISIBLE POWDER

Soviet intelligence used a unique way of keeping track of **CIA** spies in Moscow, Soviet Union. Objects that the CIA spies were likely to touch were coated with an invisible powder. The powder would then be moved onto other objects that were touched by the U.S. spies, revealing where they had been. Soviet intelligence used **ultra-violet light** to see the powder.

◄ *Checking for fingerprints. The invisible powder picked up on the spy's fingers can be seen under ultra-violet light.*

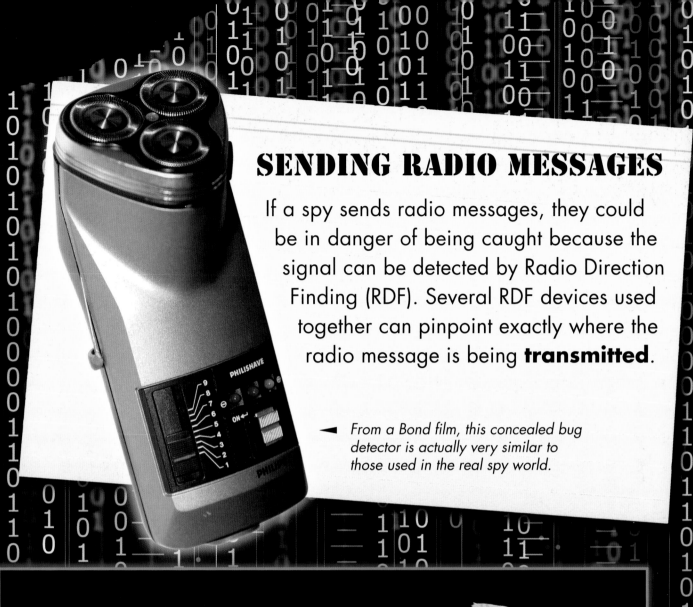

SENDING RADIO MESSAGES

If a spy sends radio messages, they could be in danger of being caught because the signal can be detected by Radio Direction Finding (RDF). Several RDF devices used together can pinpoint exactly where the radio message is being **transmitted**.

◄ From a Bond film, this concealed bug detector is actually very similar to those used in the real spy world.

THE RADIO SPY

Eli Cohen was an Israeli spy working in Syria in the early 1960s. He got to know many important people in the Syrian government and military, and sent back valuable information to Israel. Unfortunately for him, he became careless when sending radio messages and Soviet specialists tracked him down using RDF equipment. Cohen was arrested in 1965 and publicly **hanged** by the Syrians.

▲ The Israeli spy Eli Cohen (left) standing in the dock of a Syrian court. Ten days later he was **executed**.

Lie detectors

Security agencies need to know if their own spies are working for the enemy as double agents.

Spies often have to have special interviews where a lie detector, or **polygraph machine**, is used to see if they are telling the truth.

▲ The spy's pulse is being measured and recorded onto paper.

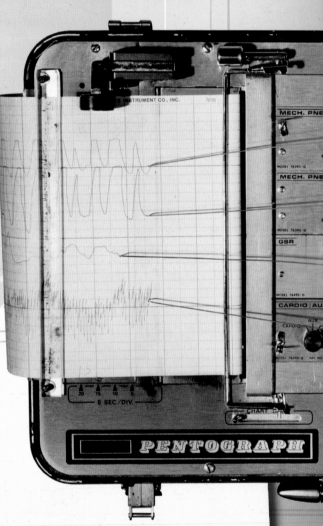

It is believed that when a person is under stress—such as when they are lying—they will show changes in their body that will give them away. In the special interview, the spy is wired up to a polygraph machine, which measures changes in **pulse**, **blood pressure** and breathing. If the spy's pulse becomes very quick, for example, it shows that they are nervous and may be lying.

18

TESTING SPIES

Polygraph tests are regularly used in spy organizations, especially in the USA. People can "fail" a test, even if they are innocent. Perhaps they feel stressed about taking the test, but they are not actually lying.

▲ A suspect takes a lie-detector test using a modern, digital polygraph machine.

BEATING THE TEST

At the beginning of a polygraph test, general questions are asked, such as "What day is it?" This sets the machine to work with the person's body. To beat the test, the person must show high stress levels at this stage. Stress levels can be raised in many ways. For example, by changing your breathing, think exciting thoughts or even biting your tongue until it hurts. Then when a difficult question is asked, such as "Are you spying for a foreign government?," the stress levels will be similar, so the person will not seem suspicious.

▲ A classic polygraph machine. Different pens mark the results onto a roll of paper.

Breaking and entering

Spies often need to enter locked houses, offices and safes.

The spy either simply steals the key, makes a copy of the key or picks the lock itself.

▲ Using two picks, a spy begins to break a simple door lock.

◄ A few of the tools required to break a lock. The different lock types require many picking tools.

LOCKS

To pick a lock takes experience and a large number of different picks. It also can take a lot of time, which puts the spy in danger of being discovered. Lock-picking machines have now been invented to make it quicker. Although the simplest and safest way is to get the right key!

MODERN METHODS

To speed up lock picking, spies often use a lock-picking gun. When a trigger is pressed, a needle pick makes the pins inside the lock line up, ready to be opened with a **tension wrench**. Electronic opening devices make the pins inside the lock move. This opens the lock without the need for more tools.

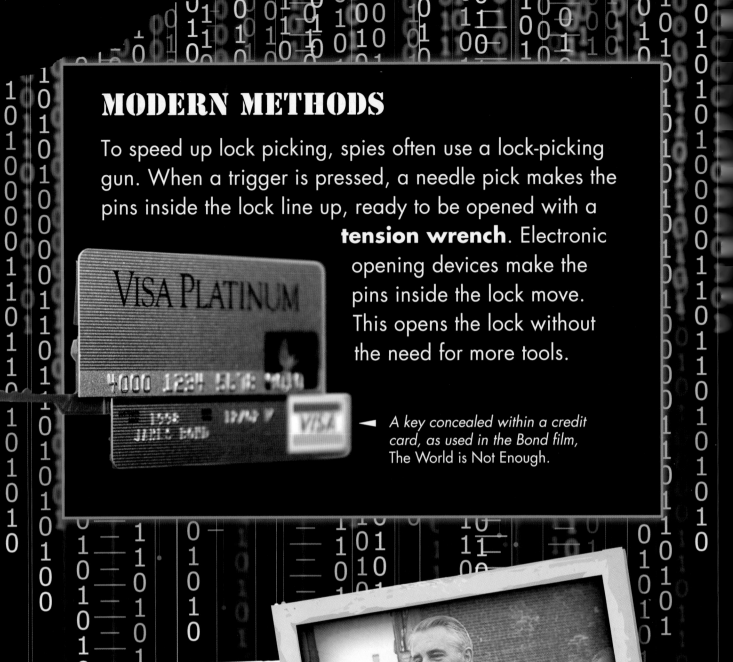

◀ A key concealed within a credit card, as used in the Bond film, The World is Not Enough.

SOVIET LOCK PICKER

In 1962, U.S. soldier Robert Lee Johnson, who worked for Soviet intelligence, was given a special **radioactive** device to break into a supposedly unbreakable safe at Orly airport near Paris, France. It took just two minutes to open the three locks.

▲ The spy Robert Lee Johnson after his arrest for espionage in 1965. He spied for the Soviets for 12 years.

Standard spy weapons

Spies normally do not carry weapons. If they were searched, the weapons would give them away.

Most spying is about finding information, not attacking or shooting. However, spies sometimes need to be armed, just in case they have to fight. Spies need weapons that are light and small enough to be hidden away in their clothing. They prefer to use police weapons because they are not as big and heavy as military weapons.

▲ An **automatic pistol** is one of the most common spy weapons. It is easy to carry and fires bullets quickly.

Top Secret!

The two automatic pistols used by James Bond were the Italian Beretta and the German Walther PPK—a more powerful weapon than the Beretta, and used by the German police service.

SILENCED WEAPONS

Although silenced weapons, usually guns, are not completely silent, the sound of a shot being fired is very quiet. The silencer also hides the **muzzle blast**—the flash from the end of the gun when the bullet has been fired.

An automatic pistol fitted with a silencer. Such weapons are only effective for close-range shooting.

Silencers are usually fitted to pistols, although they have been added to **rifles** and even sub-machine guns. Special bullets are used to stop the boom, or cracking sound, made by normal **supersonic** bullets.

CROSSBOWS

Sometimes a spy needs to use a completely silent weapon, or one that will not show a flash when fired. Then, a secret agent might use a crossbow, which is a weapon that shoots arrows. It is especially useful for killing guard dogs at night.

A modern crossbow is made ready to fire. It uses small arrows called bolts.

Close-combat weapons

A set of brass knuckle-dusters. The metal around the fingers creates a harder punch, and protects the fingers.

Sometimes, secret agents must be able to defend themselves if they are attacked face-to-face. The close-combat weapons that agents carry include coshes, knuckle-dusters, garrottes **and knives.**

These weapons are simple yet brutal. They are used when a normal weapon would be too big or noisy. Some, such as the garrotte and knife, are used to kill. Other weapons, such as the cosh and knuckle-duster, are designed to hurt and disarm the secret agent's opponent.

Top Secret!

The Soviet Union developed a single-shot pistol that was hidden within a lipstick case. It was, of course, only given to female spies!

These single-shot bullet pens were developed by the Israeli secret service.

CONCEALED WEAPONS

Spies need to hide their weapons, such as a knife strapped to their leg under their trousers. Although their weapons would be discovered if the spy were searched, most people would not notice.

EVERYDAY OBJECTS

Weapons are hidden in everyday objects that any normal person might carry, such as in cigarettes, pens, lipstick cases and even in a smoker's pipe. They are small bullets that are not very powerful, but they are capable of killing when fired a few inches from their target.

▲ A hollowed-out coin, containing a curved blade. Known as an escape coin, it could be used to slash at a captor's throat or cut ropes.

DEADLY WEAPONS

The most terrifying close-combat weapon is probably the garrotte. A length of wire is slipped around an unsuspecting person's neck — the wire is tightened and the person is strangled to death. Knives of all types are also useful for a spy because they can be hidden in clothes or shoes.

◄ This ordinary looking pair of men's shoes contains a blade that can be opened by pressing a catch on the heel.

Assassination devices

A secret service will sometimes attempt to assassinate, or kill, an enemy they think is a special threat.

Some assassinations need to be carried out without arousing suspicion, so as to make the death look like suicide or death from natural causes. One of the best assassination methods is to use poison. The Soviet Union and its **allies** were very successful at poisoning enemies.

Top Secret!

The CIA have tried to assassinate the former Cuban leader Fidel Castro at least eight times—without success!

❚ This type of umbrella was used to kill Georgi Markov. A pellet of poison was injected just under his skin.

PELLET OF POISON

Georgi Markov was assassinated in London, England, in 1978. He was jabbed in the leg by a man carrying an umbrella—he became ill, and then died the next day. At first no one knew what had happened to him, until an examination of his body showed that he had been injected with a tiny pellet of deadly poison.

▲ Georgi Markov strongly criticized the Bulgarian government, so he was assassinated.

POISONOUS TEA

In 2006, Alexander Litvinenko was poisoned—possibly by an agent of the Russian government. It is believed that Litvinenko was given the poison in a cup of tea during a meeting in a London hotel.

◀ Alexander Litvinenko lies in his hospital bed in London, England. He later died from the effects of the poison.

CELL PHONE ASSASSINATION

During the 1990s, an Islamic **terrorist** organization called Hamas began to attack Israel using bombs. Hamas' top bomb-maker was Yahya Ayyah, so he soon became an assassination target for the Israeli security forces.

The problem for the Israeli security forces was that Ayyah was closely guarded and moved from place to place all the time. They solved this by secretly giving Ayyah a cell phone, which contained a small but powerful bomb. When Ayyah made a phone call, the bomb went off and he was killed.

▲ The aftermath of a Hamas bomb blast on an Israeli bus. Israeli security forces swore to **avenge** this attack.

Sabotage

Sabotage is a way of secretly attacking an enemy country's economy—the money and goods that a country has.

This may involve blowing up railways, bridges, factories and storage plants. In the last 20 years, sabotage has also involved attacks on computer systems.

In World War I (1914–1918), German agents blew up two **ammunition** storage buildings in the United States. Although Germany was not then at war with the United States, the explosions were a way of stopping ammunition being sent to Britain and France for use in the war against Germany.

◄ Firemen put out the flames caused by German sabotage at the U.S. Black Tom ammunition depot in July 1916.

A special kit for disguising plastic explosives to look like ordinary lumps of coal.

During World War II (1939–1945), British agents sabotaged areas of Europe that were controlled by the enemy. Cunning ways were devised to carry explosives without being noticed by the Germans. **Plastic explosive** was disguised as bread, coal, stones and even animal droppings!

SOFTWARE SABOTAGE

In 1980, **KGB** Colonel Vladimir Vetrov changed from working for the Soviet Union to working for European countries in the west.

He brought with him detailed information of how Soviet spies were stealing the latest western technology. The CIA then decided to sabotage the Soviet Union.

Top Secret!

False information and booby-trapped computer technology was given to the Soviet spies. The computers seemed to work well at first but they soon caused damage to the programs.

ENORMOUS EXPLOSION

The most famous incident was the sabotage of the new trans-Siberian pipeline, which delivered gas from Siberia to countries in the west.

The surrounding area was wiped out by the Siberian gas-pipe explosion.

The CIA made sure that the program used by the Soviets to control the pipeline contained problems. At first, everything went well, until the program went wrong, causing one of the biggest explosions ever seen from space.

GLOSSARY

Allies The World War II alliance between Britain, the Soviet Union and the USA (and other, smaller countries) against Germany, Japan and Italy.

Ammunition Bullets from a gun.

Automatic pistol A hand-held weapon that fires a bullet each time the trigger is pressed, without needing to be reloaded.

Avenge To hurt or punish someone because they have harmed or offended you.

Blood pressure The pressure within the major blood vessels provided by the action of the heart. It can be used as a measure of a person's emotional state.

Capitol building The main building housing the U.S. government.

CIA Central Intelligence Agency, the intelligence-collecting organization of the USA.

Concealment Hiding something carefully.

Cosh A heavy weapon in the shape of a short, thick pipe.

Counter-intelligence The tracking down of enemy spies in one's own country.

Courier A member of a spy ring who carries secret information from place to place, usually without knowing what it is.

Double agent A spy working for two intelligence organizations at the same time. The spy is loyal to one side but only pretends to be loyal to the other.

Espionage Spying to find out information.

Exchange The act of giving something to someone and receiving something in return.

Execute To kill as punishment.

Garrotte A length of wire used to strangle someone.

Government A group of people who rule a country or state.

Hang To kill someone by hanging them with a rope around their neck.

Intelligence Information, or an organization that seeks secret information.

Intercept To stop something going from one place to another.

KGB The combined security and intelligence services of the Soviet Union.

Knuckle-duster A piece of metal that covers the knuckles of the hand — used as a weapon.

Magnification Making something look bigger than it is.

MI5 Military Intelligence Section 5, the security service of Great Britain.

Microfilm A document photographed onto film and greatly reduced in size.

Microphone An instrument for picking up sound and turning it into an electric current that can be made louder.

Military Relating to the army, navy or airforce.

Miniaturization The reduction in size of electrical objects.

Missile A rocket containing an explosive warhead.

Monocular An optical device with a single magnifying lens, instead of two as in a binocular.

Muzzle blast The flash of flame that shoots out of the end of a gun when a bullet is fired.

Plastic explosive A special explosive that can be moulded, like clay, into whatever shape is required.

Polygraph machine A machine used to find out whether someone is telling the truth.

Pulse The beating of the heart through the arteries.

Radioactive An element that releases rays that are harmful to the human body.

Radio transmitter A device for sending or broadcasting radio waves, which can be picked up by a radio receiver.

Rifle A long gun.

Soviet Union A country in Europe and Asia, between 1917 and 1991.

Supersonic Faster than the speed of sound.

Tap A special clamp placed around the phone wire so someone can listen in.

Tension wrench An L-shaped tool that helps to turn a lock open when it is being "picked."

Terrorist Someone who threatens to or uses violence, usually against civilians, to create fear and to make a government do something.

Transmit To send out radio, television or other forms of electrical signal.

Ultra-violet light A form of light that cannot be seen with the naked eye.

Unmanned aircraft An aircraft that does not have a pilot, but is controlled from the ground by an operator who usually uses a camera in the plane's nose to guide it.

Visual surveillance Watching something carefully.

INDEX